STRONG

KARA GOUCHER

strong

A RUNNER'S GUIDE TO BOOSTING CONFIDENCE
AND BECOMING THE BEST VERSION OF YOU

BLUE STAR
PRESS

BLUE STAR
PRESS

Published by Blue Star Press
PO Box 5622, Bend, OR 97708
contact@bluestarpress.com | www.bluestarpress.com

Photography by Oiselle
(unless otherwise noted below)
Page 13, 19, 25, 124/125, 206: Jess Barnard, Page 140: Joshua Rainey
Page 149: New Balance, Page 159: Kassia Meador, Page 162: Brian Kelley

Cover photo by Oiselle

Designed by Chris Ramirez

ISBN 9781944515591

Printed in China

10 9 8 7 6 5 4 3 2

DISCLAIMER:
This book is for informational and educational purposes. Please consult
your healthcare provider before beginning any exercise program.

THIS BOOK IS DEDICATED TO ANY WOMAN OUT THERE WHO HAS FELT LIKE SHE IS NOT ENOUGH. TO EVERY WOMAN WHO HAS DOUBTED HERSELF AND LACKED SELF-CONFIDENCE. YOU ARE NOT ALONE.

THIS BOOK IS FOR YOU.

contents

I BELIEVE THAT RUNNING UNITES US ALL.

Whether you're an Olympian or working toward your first 5k, we all have the same fears, doubts, and worries. I hope I inspire people to run and to stay with running even when they have setbacks, because I've been there too.

foreword

I FIRST MET KARA shortly after she graduated from the University of Colorado and for 18 years, I have had the privilege of knowing and working with her.

My first impression of Kara was that she was incredibly tough, competitive, fiercely passionate, and joyful. She stood out as a result of her remarkable grit and zest for life. To this day, my first impression of her has stood the test of time.

Working with athletes has been the primary focus of my career. When I received my master's degree, I worked at a community health center and was supervised by an astute therapist who recognized my love of sports. One of the first cases he referred to me involved a very talented yet troubled young man who happened to be a baseball superstar at his local high school. In short, he was a hotshot with a bad attitude, and his family was suffering.

While I was completing my doctoral studies at the University of

Colorado, I would play pick-up basketball after work. One day as I searched for the bathroom, preparation met opportunity when I landed in the Human Performance Lab by mistake. It was there I met my mentor of the next twenty years.

Over those years, this sage taught me about world-class athletes, and helped me to form relationships with coaches and staff in the athletic department. These relationships led me to work with many elite athletes. Eventually, I met and worked with Adam Goucher to resolve issues that he encountered as a competitive runner, and he introduced me to Kara.

My work with athletes is part therapy, part coaching, part skill-building, part strategy, and part relationship managing. Therapy is focused on finding remedies for life situations and influences in one's past. The coaching work I engage in involves assessing where the athlete is currently, anchoring their strengths, and addressing their weaknesses. I help athletes to craft goals that make sense. Most importantly, we work together to shape a game plan for how to realize their full potential.

At our first meeting, Kara was already an NCAA champion and had received a little press. When we met, Kara was experiencing a high level of stress, as well as depression. She was injured and hadn't been able to defend her NCAA title in the 5,000 meters during the spring of her senior year.

Kara downplayed her success; she was sincere, and not at all cocky. She was perhaps too modest, but full of life, quick to laugh, and very direct. She didn't know what this "therapy thing" was, but like she did everything else, she was herself, did her best, worked hard, and approached the work honestly. With Kara, what you see is what you get.

"Doing the work" is Kara's approach to everything, especially her training. She would kill workouts and training sessions, yet when we first started working together, she struggled with feeling unprepared and anxious. When it came time to race, she said she felt like an "imposter," as if she didn't belong at the starting line.

She wasted so much energy before the race started that she would be toasted halfway through. The wasting of precious energy can happen any number of ways, but is often experienced through extreme muscle tension. For any distance runner, wasting energy with muscle tension is a big problem. For Kara, it was a factor that influenced how much gas she had left in her tank before the end of a race.

Recognizing this as a problem, our initial work together focused on relaxation. Kara was already incorporating a number of techniques for building confidence into her training, and I gave her more homework to do. I asked Kara to record one good thing she did every day in her workout. It was that simple: just write down one good thing. My only criteria was that Kara write with enough precision so she could read it months later and still recall each workout.

This exercise of keeping a confidence journal evolved. Kara couldn't discount the 400 repeats and other killer training sessions she had done. Even after a tough day, she would still write down something good. Maybe it was a good shakeout or a solid warm-up, but whatever it was, Kara would emphasize the good, and let go of the rest.

Kara did her homework consistently, and a few months later, something interesting happened. The night before a meet, she reviewed her confidence journal entries and noticed that she felt calm. Her journal reminded her that she had done the work, and deserved to toe-the-line with everyone else.

Recorded consistently over time, a confidence journal can lead to a champion's mindset. It allows an individual to take ownership of their preparation, effort, and attitude toward success, one day at a time. As an everyday activity, this tool builds confidence like nothing else.

In fact, mental conditioning is increasingly recognized as an important part of an athlete's training regimen. As the level of competition continues to rise, athletes are aided by the field of exercise science, better gear, and more sophisticated coaching. While physical differences are still a factor, winning and losing are more a matter of mental preparation and toughness.

Kara's story is inspiring. It is the story of a gifted athlete, and a gifted person. As a world-class competitor and two-time Olympian, Kara has achieved incredible success in her running career, which is even more remarkable when considered against the physical challenges, injuries, mental preparation, and training that she undertook along the way.

But Kara's successes go beyond her track record. Simply put, she uses her platform in running as an expression of joy. She is amazingly inclusive of anyone who loves to run, and of anyone who is willing to give it a go. She nurtures both acceptance and personal growth. From her authentic social media presence to her Podium Retreats to the book you now hold in your hands, Kara inspires others to become the best version of themselves.

Now Kara is sharing with you everything she has learned about mental training and toughness. *Strong* includes valuable techniques for personal growth through power words, mantras, positive social connections, and more. Her voice shines as she shares her own journey. In true Kara style, she embraces the opportunity to celebrate other confident, strong women. And of course, this book also serves as a guide to the practice that has been an important aspect of Kara's running story: the confidence journal.

In *Strong*, Kara serves as a true role model in a world where such figures are hard to find. She offers a method to build confidence and character from the inside out, one day at a time.

Power and strength come from within, and this book is a worthy guide.

DR. STEPHEN WALKER,
NCC, CC-AASP, CMPC,
USOC REGISTRY OF
SPORT PSYCHOLOGY

meet the contributors

ANY BOOK HAS A TEAM of people behind the author, and *Strong* is no different. I am grateful for the advice, support, and collaboration of the many people who were involved in the development of this book. Before we start, I want to introduce you to a group of people whose expertise and perspective have been particularly invaluable. They share my belief in the importance of confidence, and that every bit of self-reflection and effort that goes into building authentic confidence will benefit and sustain you not just in your running, but for the rest of your life.

DR. STEPHEN WALKER has been my sport psychologist for years. He began his work in the field of sport and performance psychology at the Human Performance Laboratory at the University of Colorado. He is the director of Health & Sport Performance Associates in Boulder, Colorado, an adjunct professor in Sport and Performance Psychology at the University of Western States, and Editor-in-Chief of PodiumSportsJournal.com. For 19 years, he has worked to develop the use of mental conditioning skill sets with athletes from the golf, track & field, and cross-country teams.

Over the years, Dr. Walker has worked with many of the world's finest athletes (including seven Olympians from seven different sports), top coaches, and sport psychologists. In 2015, Dr. Walker's sport and performance work was nominated for the Distinguished Professional Practice Award through the Association for Applied Sport Psychology. His body of work, background in mental conditioning, use of biofeedback, and evidence-based methods in advancing the protective effects of positive emotions sets him apart as one of the top thought leaders in his field. Dr. Walker is in high demand as a consultant, coach, and public speaker, but one of his favorite roles is supporting parents who want to help their young athletes enjoy the sporting life.

ADRIENNE LANGELIER, MA, LPC began her work as a sport psychology consultant in The Woodlands, Texas, and has served as an adjunct professor in the Kinesiology Department at Sam Houston State University. Adrienne has been featured in sport-industry academic journals, the *Houston Chronicle, Daily Burn, Huffington Post,* and *Triathlete Magazine.* A passionate runner, Adrienne regularly trains and competes. She was a two-time local elite athlete for the Chevron and Aramco Houston Half Marathon, and a multiple-time qualifier for the Boston Marathon and USA Triathlon (USAT) Age Group National Championships. She currently serves as Team Captain for her racing team, the Houston Harriers.

MOLLY HUDDLE is an American long-distance runner who competes in track and cross country running events. Molly is a two-time Olympian and an American Record holder in the 10,000 meter race and the half marathon.

✶

CHRISTY TURLINGTON BURNS is a mother, global maternal health advocate, and the Founder & CEO of Every Mother Counts, a non-profit organization dedicated to making pregnancy and childbirth safe for every mother, everywhere. The organization invests in programs around the world to ensure all women have access to quality maternal healthcare. Every Mother Counts has created over 40 films to raise awareness of the global maternal health crisis including the documentary film "Every Mile, Every Mother" which explores Every Mother Counts' participation in long-distance running to highlight distance and transportation as barriers to women receiving care during pregnancy and childbirth. Christy was named one of *Glamour Magazine*'s Women of the Year in 2013, and in 2014 was one of *TIME Magazine*'s 100 Most Influential People in the World.

EMMA COBURN is a middle-distance runner who specializes in the 3,000-meter steeplechase. Emma reached the World Championships in 2011 (placing 10th) and the 2012 Olympic finals (placing 8th). She went on to win a bronze medal in the 3,000-meter steeplechase at the 2016 Olympics in Rio, making her the first American woman to win any Olympic medal in that event. Emma then became the World Champion in London in 2017. Emma has also won the IAFF Continental Cup, and is a six-time United States National Champion.

SALLY BERGESEN is the founder and CEO of Oiselle, an athletic apparel company by and for women athletes with a focus on community and design. Sally is a vocal advocate for athletes' rights and elite runner compensation, including equitable contracts for women runners. She takes a strong stand on doping and how track & field is governed. Through Oiselle, Sally supports a vibrant community of strong, competitive women who love to move, run, and fly.

ROBIN ARZÓN is *The New York Times* best-selling author of *Shut Up and Run*. Robin fearlessly left behind a successful law career to embark on new adventures in health and wellness, soon discovering her passion for coaching athletes. As Vice President of Fitness and Head Instructor at Peloton, Robin believes that sweat transforms lives. When she's not training for ultramarathons, she serves as a brand ambassador for some of the world's top fitness brands. Robin's mission in life is to redefine, reform, and rethink possibility through movement.

✱

MARY WITTENBERG was the president and CEO of New York Road Runners (NYRR) through 2015, overseeing the TCS New York City Marathon and other races, events, and programs that drew over 300,000 yearly participants. Under Wittenberg's leadership, NYRR developed new initiatives and community programs to introduce running to underprivileged children. A former competitive runner, Wittenberg won the 1987 Marine Corps Marathon. She participates in many NYRR races.

preface

THE STAKES WERE HIGH–higher than ever before. As high as they could get, really. A spot on the Olympic team was on the line. It was the night before the Olympic Trials in Los Angeles, and elite athletes were everywhere. Nerves were humming, and adrenaline was already pumping with a palpable tension in the air. A voice inside me was quiet but insistent:

"Look at them. They've beat you before.
They've been on the podium. And then there's you."

"AND THEN THERE'S YOU."

I went back to my hotel room, knowing that the country's best athletes were spending the night under the same roof.

I sat down on my bed and pulled a small, battered notebook from my bag. I had scrawled "Confidence Journal" across the cover. I smiled and thought, "You bet there's me."

* * *

I ran against the best from my country, and I didn't make the team. I wasn't going to Rio. I was just one minute and five seconds shy of my third Olympic appearance. I came in fourth, but only the top three made the team. After running at a pace of five minutes and forty-four seconds per mile, for 26.2 miles, it wasn't enough.

That night I went back to my room, exhausted and heartbroken.

I tugged my confidence journal from the nightstand and opened it to a new page. "I didn't make the cut. But I made darn sure the top three earned it."

what is a confidence journal?

ABOUT A YEAR EARLIER, my sport psychologist, Dr. Stephen Walker, suggested that I start a confidence journal. I was preparing for the 2016 Olympic Trials after having represented the United States in Beijing in 2008 and London in 2012. I certainly wasn't new to competitive running, and yet, I was realizing anew the importance of being physically and mentally prepared.

Running is a head game. When you're running, there are two options: let your mind wander or focus. To compete, you must focus. Every step, breath, and muscle movement matters for 26.2 miles. When your body is being pushed to the max, it's easy to let your mind go to a dark place, and tell you all kinds of things:

"Everyone here is better than me. I'm not ready for this. My knee hurts. Something is off."

The thing is, there are a million reasons why you can't achieve your goals. All it takes is focus and determination to find the reason you can.

For me, this is where the confidence journal started. With Dr. Walker's guidance, I began what was to become a powerful and important part of my daily training. Each day, I jotted down notes to myself about my workouts, but this was different from my training log. Rather, my confidence journal was focused purely on the positive, with the goal of building confidence.

My training log allows me to record my workouts. (I recommend the *Believe Training Journal* by my friends Lauren Fleshman and Roisin McGettigan-Dumas.) My confidence journal has a different purpose. At the end of each day, I reflect on my workout and look for something positive. I make sure that my entry is descriptive and precise so that I can read it months later and recall that workout. Some days, it comes easy. Here's my entry from September 17, 2015:

Mile repeats. The most I've ever done. With Mark and Heather as my coaches. I averaged 5:22.29. I almost lost it on mile #3 after splitting an 82 mid, and thought of failing, and almost caved, but then I thought "No. I'm Kara Goucher. If anyone can do this, I can." And then I split a 79. Great workout and the last mile was a 5:16.

At times it's much more difficult to focus on the positive, but I can always find one good thing. Here's my entry from just a few days later:

Horrible, horrible wind. Did not hit the paces I wanted, but still knocked out a solid workout. I'm definitely getting stronger.

* * *

I HAVE STRUGGLED with confidence throughout my running career. It may not be true for everyone, but I suspect it is, to one degree or another. For me, the night before a race has always been difficult. "Am I ready? Have I done enough? Did I do all the work I needed to do?" My mind would dwell on these questions.

Now, reviewing my confidence journal is part of my pre-race routine. I will actually flip through my journal to see all the times where I had great workouts and the times where

I struggled. It's a way to put it all out there on the table and realize how much work I've done, how I have prepared, and how I deserve to be competing. Even when times were hard, I still pushed through. If tomorrow's race is hard, I know I have what it takes to succeed. This practice has been so important to me, and I am excited to share it with you.

* * *

NOT JUST FOR RUNNING

I have explained how my confidence journal has influenced me as an athlete, but I think we can all benefit from a confidence journal—even outside of running. We all have our own private struggles, whether in our careers or relationships. We question all kinds of things, asking ourselves, "Am I doing it right? Have I prepared enough? What if I'm not ready? What if I'm making a mistake?" Doubt can creep into our thoughts, no matter how successful we are. What would happen if we took the time each day to quietly celebrate our accomplishments and focus on the positive? There are so many examples—in my marriage, or as a mother—where I would love to jot down something and later go back and be able to say, "Yeah. I did this right."

HOW TO BEGIN

It's one thing to just say, "You should try keeping a confidence journal!" However, I realize it can be very intimidating to open a notebook and stare at a blank page. When I first envisioned this book, I imagined that I would write a brief introduction (much like what you have read to this point) followed by some blank journal pages.

As I reflected, however, I realized that although my own confidence journal is indeed part of my daily routine, my understanding of authentic confidence took time to develop, and I had a lot of help along the way.

I realized that this book presents an opportunity to share much more about confidence: to guide you to explore why you might struggle with confidence in the first place; to learn about techniques for building confidence; and to hear a variety of perspectives from other female athletes and influencers—not just me. The final pages of this book provide prompts for reflection, and encourage you to begin your own confidence journal practice. The book you hold in your hands offers a framework of strategies to build and strengthen your confidence in a way that is personal and true to you.

Beginning to build confidence is really about asking yourself the right questions. "What did I fight through today that I didn't think I could?" Or, "What did I feel great about today? Did this surprise me?" Or perhaps, "What was the best part of today? What was the worst part, and how did I get through it?" Over time, you'll start to see that you're so much stronger than you think you are.

To say I'm grateful for running is an understatement. Running has been a source of deep joy, a means of self-discovery, a medium through which meaningful relationships have been built, and of course, running is my career. I am proud of all that I have accomplished, and I'm proud to still have goals that I'm working toward.

However, in recent years I have devoted more and more passion and energy to my retreats. It fills me with joy to encourage women to come together, to build a community focused on the positivity and beauty in running, and committed to helping each other to become our best selves—as runners and as women.

My hope is that *Strong* is a guide to becoming your best, most confident self as a runner, and in all facets of your life. I wish you all the best in your journey. 👟

confidence techniques

Developing my confidence has been a crucial component of my overall development as an elite runner. So important, in fact, that I feel motivated to share my struggles (and triumphs) with confidence to inspire others to benefit through their own "confidence building" practice. Before we dive into keeping a confidence journal, however, I want to teach you about eight different confidence techniques.

POSITIVE SELF TALK ENCLOTHED COGNITION POWER WORDS

MANTRA POWER POSE SOCIAL CONNECTIONS

SETTING GOALS VISUALIZATION TECHNIQUES *

I HAVE USED A VARIETY OF TECHNIQUES to help build my confidence, but I have never found a single "magic bullet." Rather, different techniques have worked at different points in my career. In the following section, you will explore eight techniques as you begin your own confidence-building practice. Now remember, you might immediately find value in some of these techniques; others may not seem relevant to you. I still encourage you to give each technique a chance. If a certain technique doesn't work well for you right now, it is still a valuable tool to file away. You never know—it may be useful to you at some point in the future!

The following eight mini-chapters will each focus on a single technique. Within each technique, you will read a personal story from me, accompanied by a more clinical, researched-informed perspective from my friend Adrienne Langelier, a sport psychology consultant. Each technique concludes with a "Confidence Sprint" that guides you to think about how to personalize and adapt the technique. By the time you are done, you will have developed eight new strategies for building confidence!

Before you continue, I want to emphasize two points. First, it is perfectly okay to struggle with confidence or to experience self-doubt in your running. In fact, it's quite common! Second, it's okay to talk about it. I strongly believe that these struggles should not be taboo. Being transparent and authentic (as makes sense for you) can be quite important. It can be an empowering experience to share your own story, and you never know who may benefit from hearing your truth.

I hope you enjoy learning about these techniques, and that you gain insight and skills to enhance your confidence! 🦶

I TRY TO THINK ABOUT POSITIVE THINGS—HOW GREAT MY FORM IS, HOW MY ARMS ARE SWINGING, MY BREATHING, HOW LOUD PEOPLE ARE CHEERING.

My sport psychologist taught me there are a million things telling you that you can't keep going, but if you find the things that say you can, you're golden.

✳ POSITIVE SELF TALK ✳

THE POWER OF POSITIVE SELF TALK sold me on sport psychology. Throughout my career, I had the debilitating problem of letting negative chatter cloud my head. I lined up in a race, and the destructive thoughts began: "You aren't good enough to be here. You have never run as fast as her. You have no chance. You are just a girl from northern Minnesota, and you don't belong on this big stage."

Before the race even started, I talked myself out of contention. What a stupid thing to do after all the effort and dedication I'd put into training and preparation. I knew this negativity was completely self-defeating, but I wasn't sure how to stop it. How could I stop the terrible thoughts living in my head?

With the guidance of a sport psychologist, I tried positive self talk. Instead of focusing on the reasons why I wasn't good enough, I focused on one positive reason and one thought at a time to motivate me to continue toward my goal.

In 2012, I ran the Olympic Marathon Trials in an attempt to make my second Olympic team. At that time, there was a lot going on in my head. I had suffered a severe femoral stress fracture that summer, just two months before the Trials. It took nearly five weeks with no physical activity for my leg to heal.

To top it off, I had a new coach on my first day back. To recap: I hurt my leg, didn't move for five weeks, had a brand new coach, and only had twelve days to get back into shape. I should also mention that the Olympic Trials are a full marathon—26.2 miles. Needless to say, I was out of shape and up against a wall. But I went to practice everyday, slowly climbed into decent fitness, and headed into the race convinced there was a chance I could still make it.

Positive self talk got me through that race. Every time I'd start to freak out by how out of shape I was, or how I was up against so many great women and fierce competitors, I'd refocus on something positive. One thought at a time:

"No one has broken away yet, so you've got just
as good a chance as anyone."

"Your breathing is totally controlled.
You are not running out of your league."

"Your stride is still bouncy and you have a lot left to give."

I kept telling myself these little positive nuggets as I ran. One by one, my competitors faded away. In the end, I finished third and nabbed the last Olympic spot. My dreams came true, and positive self talk made it possible.

WHAT WE SAY TO OURSELVES HAS AN INCREDIBLE IMPACT.

The happiest, most successful athletes are purposeful with their inner dialogue. They harness thoughts to work for them instead of against them through all kinds of circumstances. These athletes have learned to incorporate the use of positive, realistic self talk to help motivate and drive their performance. Anyone can change their thoughts and have control over the things they say to themselves.

My first piece of advice for athletes is to simply listen and observe what's going on above the neck. What are you saying to yourself most often? Is it positive and encouraging, such as "I'm doing amazing," or "This is all it takes!" Or, are your thoughts self-defeating, such as "There's no way I can hit these paces"?

POSITIVE IN AND POSITIVE OUT.

Changing your inner voice is a process. Here are some effective strategies to help improve your self-talk and to set yourself free from negativity.

1. **REPLACE OR REFRAME AN IDEA ABOUT YOURSELF, YOUR ABILITY, OR THE SITUATION.** For example, instead of telling yourself you're not good at running hills, tell yourself that you get stronger with every hill you run. Own your vulnerabilities and triggers, and attack them.

2. **WRITE DOWN POSITIVE STATEMENTS ABOUT YOU AND YOUR ABILITIES, AND STATE THEM CONFIDENTLY TO YOURSELF.** With enough practice and repetition, these thoughts will become dominant and replace the baseless negativity that hinders you.

3. **BE YOUR OWN FANGIRL.** Really. Talk to yourself like you talk to your best friend, or to an athlete you admire.

It's easy to fall into a pattern of being self-critical. However, while you can't change your eye color, you *can* change the voice inside your head. You can train that voice to approach the world positively. You can train it to be a loving voice that provides encouragement. It takes some time and work, but it's worth it.

FIRST, BEGIN BY WRITING THREE THINGS THAT YOU LIKE ABOUT YOURSELF. SINCE THIS IS A RUNNING BOOK, YOU MAY CHOOSE THINGS IN THE CONTEXT OF RUNNING.

Example: I'm not afraid to dream big.

NOW, WRITE THREE THINGS THAT BOTHER YOU ABOUT YOUR RUNNING.

HINT: THINK AGAIN ABOUT WHEN YOUR INNER VOICE IS CRITICAL. WHAT DOES IT SAY?

Example: Sometimes I feel overwhelmed by things, and I won't carve out enough time for running or training.

As a final step, challenge your own negative thoughts. Reframe them, and turn a "negative" statement into a positive one. This will almost certainly feel uncomfortable, but remember: discomfort can be a sign that you are learning and growing.

Let's use the example from the previous page:

Sometimes I feel overwhelmed by things, and I don't carve out enough time for running or training.

Now, here's an example of how to reframe this statement:

I have a lot of demands on my time. I'm proud of how I balance everything and still make time to train.

USE THE SPACE BELOW TO REFRAME YOUR CRITICAL THOUGHTS INTO POSITIVE THOUGHTS

1 ....
....
....

2 ....
....
....

3 ....
....
....

In my life as a runner, positive self talk has been a powerful technique. However, I have also implemented this strategy in my personal life. Training my inner voice to be patient and kind has helped me to become the best version of myself.

There's another way to begin to "train" your inner voice. Again, ask yourself if there is a core belief you struggle with. Building from there, brainstorm some positive affirmations to counteract those core beliefs. These statements can be very brief, and very direct.

Examples:

I GET BETTER. I AM ENOUGH.
I BELIEVE IN MYSELF.

USE THE SPACE BELOW TO BRAINSTORM AFFIRMATIONS:

Circle the affirmation that feels the most empowering to you. Grab a sticky note and rewrite your positive affirmation. Stick the note somewhere you will see it often: in your wallet, on your bathroom mirror, or even on the steering wheel in your car. Repeat the words to yourself whenever you see the note.

YOU CAN'T DO IN A RACE WHAT YOU HAVEN'T PREPARED FOR.

I

BELONG

MANTRA

EARLY IN MY CAREER, I struggled with doubt and anxiety about racing. Working on a mantra helped me shut out the negativity and focus on the present. One of my favorite mantras is, "I belong."

In 2007, nerves and intimidation kicked in as I stepped up with the best to run my very first World Track & Field Championship. While training for this event, I had repeated my mantra throughout tough workouts and long runs.

On race day, I kept telling myself, "I belong." That mantra helped me recall all the hard work I did to be there. Throughout the race, I repeated "I belong." When the course got tough, "I belong. I belong. I belong." I replayed these words in my head, again and again. And the mantra was true. I made it on the podium—a historical moment for me, and for the United States. The mantra I used brought me back to myself. It centered my mind and allowed me to execute the race that I knew I was capable of running.

THIS IS MY RACE STRONG
BELIEVE I AM FEARLESS

It is said that where the mind goes, the body follows. Each athlete has the power to control his or her own thoughts. One of the simplest yet most powerful ways to harness your thoughts is through using mantras. I like to refer to these words or phrases as "instruments for thinking." Mantras give athletes a mental device to sync their bodies and minds, creating focus and confidence to perform.

Not all mantras are created equal. They are often very personal and have special meaning. Different mantras can serve unique purposes, such as helping to manage discomfort, remain calm, or maintain focus.

Tips for Creating a Powerful Mantra:

- KEEP IT SIMPLE. A single word or short phrase is often sufficient. When physically pushing yourself, attempts at deep thinking or problem-solving are not advisable. Short and sweet works best.

- USE PRESENT TENSE. So much of performance is about staying in the now. Active words like "focus" and "execute" can help pull you into the moment to concentrate on the task at hand.

- ESTABLISH AN EMOTIONAL CONNECTION. A good mantra evokes positive emotions and a strong mental state. Think of words or phrases that light you up with confidence, motivation, and readiness. I find phrases like, "grit and grace" and "Why not me?" elevate me to a place where I perform my best.

- TEST YOUR MANTRA. Test out your mantras by using words and phrases in your workouts and races. If something you repeat to yourself resonates, write it down. You can also place your mantras strategically on water bottles, spike bags, shoes, or even your wrist as a reminder of your strength.

Be creative, and be consistent once you have found something that works well for you!

A mantra serves a specific purpose, and will be deeply personal. You and I could have the same mantra, but the underlying meaning of the words might be very different for each of us. Your mantra is something that you will hold on to for a long period of time. It is your mission statement. I think it's also important to realize that if your mantra no longer inspires you or excites you, then it may be time to develop a new one.

The following exercise will help you discover a meaningful and powerful mantra. A mantra is your purpose. It's okay to take your time and test different words and phrases. You will know when you have found the right one, as it will deeply resonate with you.

THIS IS MY RACE
I AM FEARLESS
I BELONG

LIST THREE RECURRING WORRIES THAT HOLD YOU BACK:

....
....
....

....
....
....

3

....
....
....

Example of a constant worry of mine:

"I DON'T THINK I'M GOOD ENOUGH TO COMPETE AT THIS RACE."

**NOW, WRITE THREE PHRASES THAT ARE THE OPPOSITE OF
THE "WORRY PHRASES" YOU BRAINSTORMED:**

 1 ....
....
....

2 ....
....
....

3 ....
....
....

Examples of opposite "worry phrases":

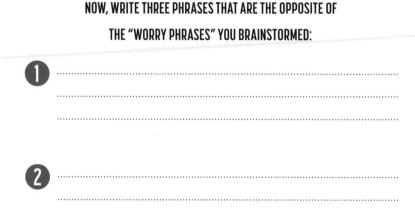

I BELONG AT THIS RACE

YES I CAN I AM STRONG

CONSIDER SOME OF THE THINGS YOU STRUGGLE WITH.
AS YOU DO SO, BRAINSTORM WORDS THAT YOU FIND INSPIRING OR EMPOWERING.

Here are some inspiring words to help get you started:

If you strive for self-love, some of your words could be

BELONG   CONFIDENT   WORTHY

If you struggle with anxiety, try to think of words like:

CALM   AT EASE

If you struggle with motivation, try words like:

DETERMINED   SPARK

WRITE YOUR OWN WORDS IN THE SPACE BELOW:

....

....

....

....

....

....

....

....

SET SMALL GOALS ALONG THE WAY AND DON'T BE OVERWHELMED BY THE PROCESS.

---·--- *SETTING GOALS* ---·---

WHEN I WAS YOUNGER I did not like to verbalize my goals.
What if I said, "I want to be state champion in the 3,200 meters
and run under 10 minutes and 40 seconds" and then that didn't
happen? What if I failed to achieve the goal that others knew I
was working for? "Wouldn't it be terrible," I thought, "wouldn't
it be horrible and embarrassing if I wanted something so bad
and admitted it and then didn't get it after telling everyone I
would?"

As I got older, I shifted away from that line of thinking. I learned
that there are different types of goals. Some are smaller and
build on each other. Then there are bigger goals, those pie-in-
the-sky ones. It's important to know that the little goals help
you get to the big goals.

In 2009, I set the goal of winning the Boston Marathon. This was
a BIG goal, and I shared it with the world. I knew that I really
wanted it, and I was going to do everything I could to achieve
it. After setting the goal to win Boston, I had to set little goals

to help me along the way. For instance, I set the goals to run eight weeks of one hundred miles or more, to get my long run up to 24 miles, and to maintain my speed with track sessions every other week so I would still be able to sprint when I got to Boylston Street—the finish line.

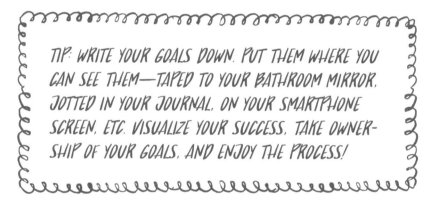

TIP: WRITE YOUR GOALS DOWN. PUT THEM WHERE YOU CAN SEE THEM—TAPED TO YOUR BATHROOM MIRROR, JOTTED IN YOUR JOURNAL, ON YOUR SMARTPHONE SCREEN, ETC. VISUALIZE YOUR SUCCESS, TAKE OWNERSHIP OF YOUR GOALS, AND ENJOY THE PROCESS!

Running a hundred miles or more a week for eight weeks was an easy goal to track, as was working my long run up to 24 miles. I held myself accountable on keeping my speed up by running (and winning) the women's mile at the Millrose Games, and the 3,000 meters at the Boston Indoor Games. Meeting these little goals along the way helped grow my confidence as I headed to the Boston Marathon.

Unfortunately, I didn't win the Boston Marathon in 2009. I lost in a sprint over the final mile, and faded to third place. To say that I was devastated is an understatement—but I never regretted sharing my goal with the world. I wanted to win. Nothing less would satisfy me, so why not just go for it? Setting goals allowed me to stay the course, follow the journey, and work for what I wanted from my running.

It was hard to get over, but I was finally able to move on. I started by setting a new goal. And that's the best part, really: there is always a new goal to work toward. 🏃

THERE IS BOTH A SCIENCE AND AN ART TO SETTING IDEAL GOALS FOR AN INDIVIDUAL ATHLETE.

I believe that a good goal is both inspiring and a touch scary (in a positive sense, of course). A solid personal goal is challenging, but not overwhelming. Well-considered and executed, long and short-term goals can be conduits for growth. Individualized, attainable goals can instill confidence, and will often be building blocks for great success.

Let's look at some of the considerations and processes of goal-setting that inspire confidence. Note that setting goals is a very individual process. Be sure to take ownership of your goals, and believe in your ability to carry them out. Consider these components as you set your goals:

ATTAINABILITY. Is what you want to do—say qualifying for Boston—in line with your current ability and fitness level? Remember the "challenging but not overwhelming" principle. Attainability is important to consider when setting yourself up for success.

TIME-ORIENTATION. Having a reasonable working deadline helps you with the process of achieving your goals. Make sure you allow enough time for the process and for your fitness to develop. Identifying and achieving your goal should not be rushed.

ADJUSTABILITY AND FLEXIBILITY. Being rigid is not always helpful. Setting a range of goals can be a great path.

INSPIRATIONAL. Think about how you want to feel when you cross the finish line, or when you accomplish your goal.

PROCESS-FOCUSED. Be mindful of the steps it takes to get to where you want to go. Include the little things, such as recovery and mental training. Break your goals into manageable steps. It can be helpful to set a "big picture" or long-term goal, and then identify short-term goals to keep you motivated.

I set goals for myself. It's what I do and who I am. As long as I can remember, I have always had something that I am working toward.

Of course, I haven't always achieved my goals, though it has never been from a lack of effort, and I have learned a thing or two along the way. First, if you set a BIG goal (and you should), you're going to need a solid plan in place. Second, that plan can almost always be broken down into smaller goals that serve as milestones along the way. This can help to keep you motivated and focused as you work toward what you want to achieve. Let's break this down:

WHAT IS YOUR BIGGEST LONG-TERM GOAL, RUNNING OR OTHERWISE?

....

....

....

....

....

....

....

....

IS YOUR GOAL ATTAINABLE?

YES   MAYBE   NO

If you circled **YES**: GREAT! Let's get to planning!

+ + + +

If you circled **MAYBE**: that's okay, too! A "maybe" goal often just needs some proper perspective and planning to really become achievable. We'll get to that below.

If you circled **NO**: consider rethinking this goal. It's smart to set yourself up for success. Remember, smaller successes are building blocks to greater success. Reframe your goal and think about something that will challenge you, but that is still achievable with dedicated time and effort.

NOW THAT YOU HAVE CLEARLY IDENTIFIED YOUR GOAL, CONSIDER WHY THIS GOAL IS IMPORTANT TO YOU. WHAT IS YOUR MOTIVATION?

....

....

....

....

....

....

....

....

WHAT TIME FRAME DO YOU FEEL IS REASONABLE TO ATTAIN THIS GOAL? REMEMBER, REACHING YOUR GOAL PROBABLY WON'T HAPPEN OVERNIGHT—AND THAT'S OKAY!

....

....

....

....

....

....

....

....

....

Pause for a moment. Close your eyes and envision what it will be like when you achieve your goal. Now think about the milestones you will hit on your way toward your goal. What are they?

BREAK THINGS INTO THREE SMALLER, MANAGEABLE (AND MEASURABLE) GOALS:

1 ....
....
....

2 ....
....
....

3 ....
....
....

You have a plan, and you're on your way. Starting TODAY, what is your first step toward achieving your goal? Get out there and get after it. I believe in you!

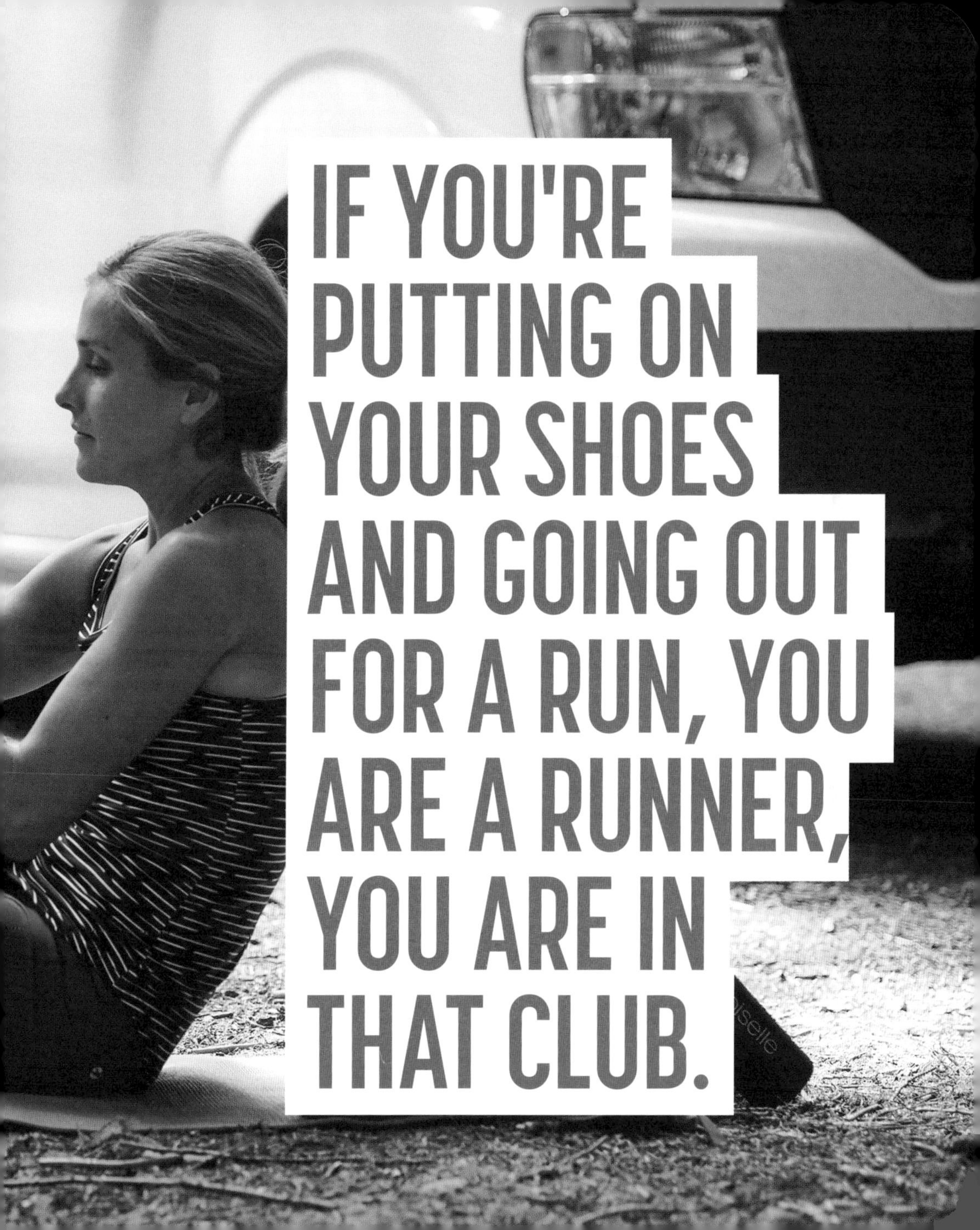

IF YOU'RE PUTTING ON YOUR SHOES AND GOING OUT FOR A RUN, YOU ARE A RUNNER, YOU ARE IN THAT CLUB.

THE POWER OF CLOTHES

 ENCLOTHED COGNITION

ENCLOTHED COGNITION IS AN IMPORTANT TECHNIQUE I use to boost my confidence. The term refers to how the clothes you wear can affect your mental and physical performance. Now, I have a lot of running clothes, but it may surprise you that there are certain clothes I only wear for tough training sessions, and others I wear just on race days.

The pieces I wear on challenging training days fit me a certain way and when I feel the fabric hug my skin, I know it's game time. Just feeling the clothes on my body helps me focus on the task ahead. It's as if the clothes command my mind to dig a little deeper and truly go the extra mile.

When I slide into my uniform on the morning of a race, I feel an extra layer of invincibility. It's as if my uniform turns me into my own superhero, and I can achieve anything. I warm up in special clothes, and my body and mind know that the time is now. This is what I have been waiting and training for.

Again, just the feeling of these clothes signals to my mind and body that the wait is over and it's time to go out and achieve what I have worked so hard for. The power of these clothes is incredible and they steer my body and mind into a place of absolute determination.

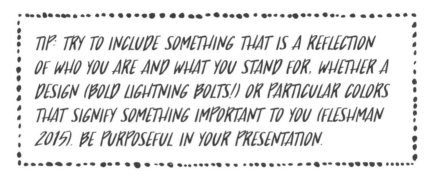

TIP: TRY TO INCLUDE SOMETHING THAT IS A REFLECTION OF WHO YOU ARE AND WHAT YOU STAND FOR, WHETHER A DESIGN (BOLD LIGHTNING BOLTS!) OR PARTICULAR COLORS THAT SIGNIFY SOMETHING IMPORTANT TO YOU (FLESHMAN 2015). BE PURPOSEFUL IN YOUR PRESENTATION.

ENTRIES FROM MY CONFIDENCE JOURNAL

9/20   BIG TEX. I've struggled the last two times I ran here, but I nailed it. Was surprised by how fast and relaxed I was running for first 4. Forgot the urge to panic and slow. Great overall average, great day.

11/17   Horrible horrible wind. But still knocked out a solid 20x200 in 34— Getting stronger and faster.

PSYCHOLOGISTS USE ENCLOTHED COGNITION TO DRIVE AT THE IDEA THAT WHAT WE WEAR AFFECTS HOW WE THINK, HOW WE PERFORM, AND OF COURSE, OUR LEVEL OF CONFIDENCE.

If we think about it, it makes sense. Can you recall a time when you wore a new singlet and crushed your PR, or nailed a presentation at a board meeting in your favorite suit? You probably walked more confidently that day. That's enclothed cognition at work.

A study even found that those wearing a doctor's coat were more attentive and showed better all-around performance on a task than those not wearing one (Adam & Galinsky 2012). Why? Two factors appear to combine and influence the mental state of the wearer: the symbolic meaning of the clothes and the physical experience of wearing them. The clothes mean something to you, and you feel good wearing them. I would personally argue a race kit is every bit as powerful as a lab coat.

As an athlete, the clothing you wear may indicate who you run for, such as your team or sponsor. Or, it may simply be a backdrop for your racing bib. Perhaps it just feels fast. When I put on my race kit, I feel the importance of being part of a team, and everything that means to me.

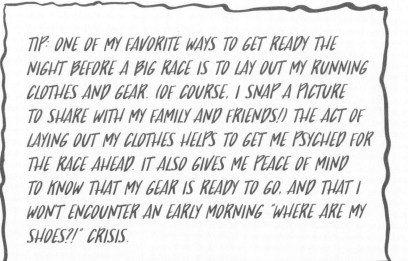

TIP: ONE OF MY FAVORITE WAYS TO GET READY THE NIGHT BEFORE A BIG RACE IS TO LAY OUT MY RUNNING CLOTHES AND GEAR. (OF COURSE, I SNAP A PICTURE TO SHARE WITH MY FAMILY AND FRIENDS!) THE ACT OF LAYING OUT MY CLOTHES HELPS TO GET ME PSYCHED FOR THE RACE AHEAD. IT ALSO GIVES ME PEACE OF MIND TO KNOW THAT MY GEAR IS READY TO GO, AND THAT I WON'T ENCOUNTER AN EARLY MORNING "WHERE ARE MY SHOES?!" CRISIS.

Do you have a favorite outfit that you wear for important days? Maybe something you wear for a big day at work? What do you love about that outfit? Does it make you feel put together, or like you can handle anything? We all have favorite articles of clothing such as a pair of jeans that fits just right, a sweater that is especially cozy, or a power suit that says, "Don't mess with me!"

THINK ABOUT SOME OF YOUR STRONGEST RACE OR TRAINING DAYS. WHAT WERE YOU WEARING? (YOU CAN LOOK AT RACE PHOTOS OR SOCIAL MEDIA TO JOG YOUR MEMORY.) WERE YOU INTENTIONAL ABOUT CHOOSING YOUR CLOTHES FOR THAT DAY? HOW DID THEY MAKE YOU FEEL?

DO YOU PREFER TO WEAR LOOSE OR TIGHT CLOTHING WHEN YOU RUN? HOW DOES THE FIT AFFECT HOW YOU FEEL?

(Example: tight clothing may make you feel sleek and fast, especially on a cold, windy day. In contrast, light, loose clothing may be your option on sweltering summer days.)

....

....

....

....

....

....

....

DO YOU HAVE FAVORITE GO-TO BRANDS? CERTAIN SOCKS THAT YOU LIKE BEST FOR LONG RUNS? A PARTICULAR HAIRSTYLE YOU LIKE TO ROCK?

....

....

....

....

....

....

....

I wear running clothes for at least part of almost every day. You better believe that I have my favorites. With some pieces, it's the color. With others, it's the fit. I have certain items of running clothing that I associate with a special memory. My version of a "power suit" is the running clothes that help me to bring my best, most prepared, most confident self to my running.

Another thing to consider: color is extremely powerful. Certain colors even have the power to evoke emotional responses.

ARE THERE SPECIFIC COLORS YOU ARE DRAWN TO? WHY?
DO THESE COLORS MAKE YOU FEEL A CERTAIN WAY?
ARE THEY COLORS THAT APPEAR IN YOUR RUNNING WARDROBE?

....

....

....

....

....

....

....

....

Now that you know what enclothed cognition is, jot some notes about the outfits you might like to wear for each type of run:

EASY DAY

....

....

....

....

LONG RUN DAY

....

....

....

....

SPEED WORK DAY

....

....

....

....

RACE DAY

....

....

....

....

DO THE WORK.
DO THE ANALYSIS.
BUT FEEL YOUR
RUN. FEEL YOUR
RACE. FEEL THE
JOY THAT IS
RUNNING.

I MEAN BUSINESS.

» POWER POSE «

POWER POSES WORK BEST FOR ME right on the starting line. Whether at a workout or race, I feel confident and ready to execute the task ahead if I begin by standing focused and calm at the start.

Years ago, I had a coach tell me to "Be a pirate!" While this does conjure a hilarious mental image, the point of his advice was this: even pirates get scared when they go out to do their pirate thing. They're facing death, after all! But they go anyway. They face their fears, and do what they are there to do. So when I'm about to run a race, it's okay to feel scared—as long as I go out and do what has to be done.

When I look at photos of myself on the starting line, I am always standing tall and looking straight ahead. While others move around, shaking their legs and arms, I choose to stand still. I didn't realize that "power pose" was the term for this until a few years ago, but it's something I have done throughout my entire career. Those last few seconds before a race can be frantic. I hate that feeling, that lack of control. I've always hated it. But through my power pose, I found a way to take back control and prepare to race.

As one of the shorter girls in high school, I'd stand firm and look ahead. It made me feel like I knew a secret. In a way, I did. Unlike the other girls on the line, I wasn't wasting any energy. I was ready to use it all on the course or track. Now that I'm one of the taller women out there, I like it even more. I tower over everyone and feel as solid as a rock. This pose gives me strength and sends the message to everyone else that I mean business. In my head, I am convinced that I can leave the line feeling more calm and confident than anyone I am competing against. ✦

ENTRIES FROM MY CONFIDENCE JOURNAL

10/8   Huge day! 10x1K in 3:15. Nailed
         it and even accelerated at the end.
         Feeling fitter. Averaged 3:14 but
         last two were 3:13 and 3:11.

10/12   Hard windy day. So windy! 23
         total w/ middle 15 doing 2 miles
         @ race pace and then 1 steady.
         A little slow overall, but really
         worked the last set hard, so never
         gave in.

IF YOU WERE THE BEST ATHLETE YOU COULD BE, HOW WOULD YOU LOOK AND ACT?

Confidence radiates from the inside out. But can it also come from the outside in? Did you know we can "talk" to ourselves using nonverbal cues? Research in behavioral science seems to think so. According to psychologist Amy Cuddy and her compelling study, our body language affects how we see ourselves and interact with the environment around us (Carney, Cuddy, & Yap 2010).

In moments where you want to feel more confident and strong, try adjusting your posture to be bigger, outstretched, present, and open. Holding your posture in a powerful manner for a period of just one to two minutes can positively change your risk tolerance and how you react to stress (Carney, Cuddy, & Yap 2010). The more we radiate messages like, "Bring it on," or "I'm ready," the more our thoughts follow our posture. Knowing this, wouldn't you move a little braver throughout the world?

Keep your head up and eyes forward. To feel more powerful, pay attention to your head and eye position. Both head and eyes should be facing forward, with shoulders square and open, and your spine straight (but not so much it feels unnatural). Also, smiling gives your brain extra positive feedback without saying a word. You know that point in a race when it's no longer fun? Try a small smile or running a little taller as a subtle way to remind yourself, "I can do this."

TIP: PERIODICALLY CHECK IN WITH WHAT YOUR BODY LANGUAGE IS SAYING. PRACTICE OPENING YOURSELF UP AND MOVING WITH PURPOSE, REGARDLESS OF HOW YOU FEEL IN THE MOMENT. YOU CAN ALSO PUT THIS INTO PRACTICE BY DISPLAYING YOUR STRENGTH AS YOU WALK TO THE STARTING LINE, TAKING OWNERSHIP OF YOUR RACE.

You may be asking yourself, "Why am I writing about a physical pose? That seems odd!" Even though a power pose is something you do physically, it helps me to think and write about how I might want to use a power pose in my running.

SO LET'S GET INTO IT!

THINK ABOUT YOURSELF AT THE START OF A RECENT RACE OR LONG TRAINING RUN. DESCRIBE HOW YOU FELT AND LOOKED:

....

....

....

....

....

....

....

....

....

....

....

....

Now, think about how you *want* to feel when you get ready for a race or a big run. Again, close your eyes. Try to visualize how you would like to feel, and how you would like for this to translate physically.

WHEN YOU'RE READY, DESCRIBE HOW YOU WOULD LIKE TO LOOK AND FEEL HERE:

....

....

....

....

....

....

....

....

....

....

....

....

Practice makes perfect. Find a mirror and practice your power pose. Remember, you are strong and confident. And you are ready to kick some butt! Take your power pose out for a spin the very next chance you get.

ERASE FROM YOUR MIND THAT YOUR PREPARATION MUST BE PERFECT. HARD WORK + DEDICATION = A SHOT AT YOUR DREAMS. KEEP BELIEVING.

VISUALIZATION TECHNIQUES

WHEN I WAS IN COLLEGE, my coach had our cross country team lay down on the ground. He told us to close our eyes and run the national cross country championship course in our head. When we finished, we would sit up and see how long it took to run the race. I was the first one to sit up after about 30 seconds. Not exactly what my coach had in mind.

I've learned that visualization works best for me when I am out and running. I imagine myself not in training, but in the race itself. I picture what the course or track looks like and what it will feel like to close those last few miles or to sprint that last bend of the track. This practice of visualization helps me get the nerves out, picture the day, and make a connection between the act of running and competing at my best.

I visualize outside of running too, often at night as I fall asleep. I always try to imagine myself strong, connected to my body. It's here that I visualize what I would do if something went wrong, if I tripped or missed a water bottle at an aid station in a marathon. I end by dealing with the situation calmly, and not letting it affect my mental state.

You can visualize while laying down, during your run, or whatever else that works best for you. The important thing is to be able to see yourself achieving what you wish to accomplish, a "practice run" of what is to come. 🏃

ENTRIES FROM MY CONFIDENCE JOURNAL

9/2   workout 14x500. I stayed patient at the beginning and didn't try to rush it, leaving myself ready to tackle the last few with energy to spare.

9/4   12 mile tt. HR was much lower than last time. Never felt like I was at the edge—had plenty left.

TO FULLY REACH YOUR POTENTIAL, YOU MUST FIRST BE ABLE TO SEE IT IN YOUR MIND'S EYE.

According to studies, proper use of visualization and imagery has been shown to increase endurance performance and muscle memory without the extra pounding of mileage (McCormick, Maijen, & Marcora 2015). For athletes, using visualization effectively takes some practice and direction. You are reprogramming your brain to perform. Visualization can be used to refine technique or race strategy, prep for big workouts, help to manage nerves, or to build confidence by seeing a successful finish long before you get to the starting line.

Here are some keys to using this powerful mental weapon effectively:

- **BE CONSISTENT.** Set aside time to mentally rehearse. Relax with your eyes closed and your mind focused on the nuances of your race and/or key workouts. Schedule this time in your training if you need to.

- **ALWAYS END YOUR SESSION POSITIVELY.** See and feel yourself performing well in your mind's eye.

- **BE PATIENT WITH YOURSELF IF YOU DON'T GET IT RIGHT AWAY.** Positive neural pathways are strengthening each session, wiring together over time.

Along with seeing a strong start and an even stronger finish while hitting your goals along the way, don't forget to also work through scenarios where you tend to struggle. For example, do you fall off pace during the middle miles? Visualize yourself relaxing and responding appropriately to these challenging times. This isn't necessarily comfortable, but do it enough and the right response in a difficult situation can become automatic.

As always, be creative in your visualization practice. Seeing really is believing.

Since I've written a book about the importance of building confidence in running, you already know that I'm a firm believer in the importance of mental training and preparation. Visualization is a technique that can feel awkward at first. It's okay to think that, but trust me and give this a try. If visualizing your run isn't something you've done before, I think you will be surprised by the experience.

VISUALIZATION EXERCISE #1

1. First, it's important to designate a quiet place and time when you can eliminate distractions. Perhaps this is while your kids are at school during the day, or early in the morning before your partner wakes up and your workday begins.

2. Find a comfortable (or even a not-so-comfortable) place to lie down. Even the floor will do!

3. Close your eyes and begin to take deep, even breaths. Feel the oxygen travel in through your nostrils and fill your lungs. Hold at the top of your breath for just a moment

before you slowly exhale. Take a few minutes and allow your breathing to help relax your body.

4. Now you are ready. Begin by visualizing a real-life scenario. Perhaps you are picturing yourself at the beginning of a long training run, or at the beginning of your next race. In your mind's eye, be as realistic as you can. See yourself taking a last sip of water, checking your laces, or stretching your calves and hamstrings. Do you feel butterflies? Do you feel excited and eager to start your run?

5. Taking your time, mentally go through your run. Try to engage all of your senses. When do you begin to feel thirsty? Is there a moment when you start to cramp? Does the air smell fresh? Is the weather brisk, or sweltering?

6. Visualize yourself finishing your run strong.

How did your "run" feel? Did you have any emotions come up during your visualization session? Did you encounter anything unexpected? Take a moment to write down some thoughts about your "run."

VISUALIZATION EXERCISE #2

If you are like me and visualizing while laying down or sitting quietly just isn't your style, then you should try the following exercise.

1. Head out on an easy run. Keep your eyes open, get into your groove, and then start your visualization exercise.

2. Now, I want you to focus on a challenging part of your run. Perhaps this is a hill that just *kills* you every time. Perhaps you hate the feeling when a competitor is nipping at your heels. Perhaps you struggle mightily with nerves at the beginning of a race. Whatever it is, take your mind there. Lean into the image. Allow yourself to be mentally uncomfortable as you visualize that experience.

3. Now, begin to imagine strategies to help you power through your own personal challenging scenario. Picture yourself at the starting line taking deep breaths, feeling calm and ready to start your race. Imagine taking that hill slow and steady, one step at a time, and still having energy left when you get to the top.

What came up during this visualization session? Do you feel less nervous and more prepared for what you may encounter?

The fact of the matter is that running is not for the faint of heart. I think those of us who run also secretly (or perhaps not secretly) love the challenge. We like to push ourselves and test our limits. If you share the feeling, you probably already know that in running, you encounter tough and unpredictable moments. You can combat these uncomfortable moments by preparing with visualization. Then, if or when you encounter this situation, you know you can handle it because you have already conquered it through visualization.

This is an intense technique. Depending on your needs, it may be one you want to use as much as 2-3 times a week. Or, it may be most helpful when you are preparing for a bigger run or race. Either way, keep this technique in your pocket. Visualization is a very powerful tool.

I HAVE A POWER WORD THAT I USE—WHEN I QUALIFIED FOR THE OLYMPICS IN 2008, IT WAS "FIGHTER".

⋛≪ *POWER WORDS* ≫⋚

I LOVE USING POWER WORDS as a technique for building up my confidence. For a power word to truly work, you must practice using it in everyday situations so you will be able to draw on its full power come race day.

I've used many power words over the years. Typically, I pick a word at the start of a training cycle. In 2008, I decided to run my first marathon and I was nervous. Could I handle the training? Could I stay injury-free? Could I even run that far?

The word I picked for that cycle was "courage." I found the courage to test myself to the ultimate limit, believe in myself, and push past self-doubt.

Throughout the eight weeks between my Olympic 5,000-meter final and the start of the New York City Marathon, I constantly told myself that I was courageous. On the day I first ran 18 miles, I was tired and scared, but I kept telling myself that I would get through it. On days where I had breakthrough practices like my first twenty-miler and longest mileage week, I repeated the word "courageous" to myself. And on those days when I faltered and couldn't hit the times I wanted, I continued to remind myself that I was courageous simply for trying.

I was a bundle of nerves the night before the marathon. The pressure and expectations mounted—and I still didn't know if I could even run 26 miles. As I lined up the next morning, I kept whispering to myself that I was courageous. By this time, I had practiced this message to myself so many times in training that I could relate it to times when I felt powerful, or when I had survived the stickiest situations. This allowed the word "courage" to continuously run through my head during the marathon, and helped me to push through the biggest accomplishment of my life: finishing a marathon.

Not only did I finish, but I placed third and ran 2:25:53, which still stands as the fastest time an American woman has run on the New York City Marathon course. 🏃

ENTRIES FROM MY CONFIDENCE JOURNAL

8/9   Feeling really bad and stiff from traveling. Doing 3x1 Mile laps and after 2 had option to stop. Decided to go and ended up fastest one!

9/17   Mile repeats. The most I've done for Mike and Heather! Average 5:22:09. Almost lost it on mile #3 after splitting 82 mid, thought of failing and almost caved but then thought "NO! I'm KG. If anyone can do this I can!" Then split 79. Great workout, last mile in 5:16:08.

IT'S YOUR LAST REP IN A SET OF KILLER MILE REPEATS.

Your lungs are searing, your legs and arms are heavy. Coming into the final 400 meters, your inner voice practically shouts the words "Smooth!" and "Focus!" Suddenly, your perceived effort drops just enough as you execute your assigned pace.

What you did was not easy, but you chose your words wisely and finished strong.

Power words are one of my go-to confidence-building techniques. These words can help you reduce distractions (like negative self talk) and focus on what you're doing right now. These words are short, positive, personal, and refreshingly simple. It's useful to have a simple strategy such as incorporating a positive cue word or two to get through a difficult task and refocus.

For the best results, choose words that are personal. They need to be believable and relevant to your style and situation.

What works for you may not work for a friend, or vice versa. Obviously, the words need to be positive and inspire confidence and motivation. Remember, the body follows the mind, and it's more likely to respond if given specific instructions. Don't forget: these words or phrases should be brief and easy to remember. In the heat of the moment, we need our go-to words to be easily accessible. I like to tell my athletes that you have the right verbiage when you consistently tell yourself what you want and need to hear in key moments of a race or workout.

Here are some examples:

PRECISE EXECUTE FAST

EFFORTLESS LIGHT SMOOTH

GRIT FRESH BEAUTIFUL

POWERHOUSE GRACEFUL FEEL

DRIVE KICK FREE

At first a mantra and a power word might seem almost identical. And it's true that they are very similar. Remember, your mantra reflects your mission—your deep, underlying personal reason for doing what you do. On the other hand, power words are quick, impactful words that are used for moments, specific races, or specific days. On a day with a speed workout, your power word might be "Fight." On a long run day, an effective power word might be "Endure."

First, you'll need a pen and timer (I use the timer on my phone) for this exercise.

SET THE TIMER TO FIVE MINUTES. WRITE ANY AND EVERY WORD THAT INSPIRES YOU, EMPOWERS YOU, OR SIMPLY MAKES YOU FEEL HAPPY:

....

....

....

....

....

....

....

....

....

....

Look at the words you just brainstormed. Set your timer for another five minutes. Consider each word, and circle your top ten words. There is no particular set of criteria you need to adhere to as you choose your words. Trust your gut, and select the ten words that are the most meaningful to you.

Now, narrow things down even more. Of the ten words you circled, draw a line through the five words that appeal to you the least.

The words that remain are your top five power words.

WRITE YOUR TOP FIVE WORDS HERE:

1 ....

2 ....

3 ....

4 ....

5 ....

Now that have your list of words, it's time to use them. Use your power words during training, during a race, or anytime you need an extra boost of motivation. I would love to know what you come up with.

USE

#STRONGWITHKARA

AND SHARE YOUR WORDS WITH ME ON INSTAGRAM AND TWITTER

@KARAGOUCHER

SEE OTHER COMPETITORS AS YOUR FRIENDS.

Your only real competitor is yourself. The idea is to beat the distance, not the person next to you. So hang in there, stay positive, and take in the positive energy from everyone around you.

SOCIAL CONNECTIONS

THE CONFIDENCE I HAVE GAINED through my supportive social connections has contributed directly to my success. My connections with my training partners and coaches help me to feel self-worth and confidence. They see me on my best and worst days. They see me nail workouts, but they also see me suffer, leaving the track in tears after a hard day.

And I also see them. I see my training partner's confidence dip when she doesn't hit a workout she set out to complete, and I see her move toward her goal after an incredible long run.

When I am connected to others and their success, I am invested in them. I want them to do well and achieve all that they have set out to do. When they have a good day, I ride that high with them. When they have a bad day, I am there to encourage them. This goes both ways, and the support I give comes back to me.

Additionally, when I see my partners succeed, I know that I can do the same. We have been through so much together, and my joy in watching friends and partners race gives me confidence in my own journey. It is truly a symbiotic relationship in which the investment we make in one another builds us up together. 🦶

ENTRIES FROM MY CONFIDENCE JOURNAL

9/25   4x10 min on 15 off—still a little
        sore from Philly but ran hard
        and solid. Nailing marathon pace.
        Nothing glamorous just good work.

10/19   Amazing 18 mile run and 1
        cooldown. Literally had to hold
        myself back at times and never
        slowed a bit. In the
        last 1/3 of run—in fact gained time
        there. 6:07 average and HR 156.
        So close to being ready.

RUNNING IS A POWERFUL VEHICLE FOR BONDING.

As women and athletes, we gain strength when we gather together. Numerous studies have found that connecting with others, even in the smallest ways, can help prevent burnout, increase self-esteem, and strengthen the ability to cope with adversity, such as injuries and setbacks (Petrie, Deiters, & Harmison 2014). Our relationships with others can also help us to build confidence and mental toughness (Gabana, Steinfeldt, Wong & Chung 2016). In short, a community of women makes us stronger.

What is it about connecting with others that psychologically elevates us? For starters, common experience—the pain, the commitment, the joy—is powerful. Building up and being built up operates two-fold when it comes to growing confidence. Social connections cause chemical changes in your brain, providing a hit of positive emotion and confidence.

Need to be uplifted? Here are some strategies:

RUN WITH THOSE WHO KEEP YOU ACCOUNTABLE. A good running partner can help you make wise training decisions and provide just enough push.

HANG OUT IN THE LIGHT. Spend most of your time and energy with those who make you feel good about yourself. Why spend time with those who invite comparison or negativity?

BELIEVE IN OTHERS AND BELIEVE IN YOURSELF. When you're training and racing, think about those who have helped you along the way. Do they believe you can do it? Then you should, too.

HELP OTHERS. Find ways to show your support at races, charity events, or other causes you care about.

MENTOR A YOUNGER OR LESS EXPERIENCED RUNNER. This does wonders for confidence—both theirs and yours.

Also, remember that social connections don't have to be much to be effective. Sometimes a smile, a word of encouragement, or a simple, "You're doing great!" during a race goes a long way.

Study after study has shown that the strength of social connections directly correlates to general happiness. In my own life, I make it a priority to nurture my connections with family and friends. These include the strength of connections in my running family, where my bonds with my training partners have stood the test of time.

Running can certainly be a solitary sport. In fact, for many people, that's part of the appeal. It's easy to lace up your shoes and just go. However, running communities can also be a powerful source of support and connection. They can offer accountability and encouragement. Fellow runners can be very grounding in an otherwise hectic life. I know a number of people who have commented that they spend more quality time with their running partners than with almost anyone else in their lives.

WHO ARE THE PEOPLE IN YOUR LIFE THAT SUPPORT, INSPIRE, AND ENCOURAGE YOU? THINK ABOUT THE PEOPLE WHO INFLUENCE YOU IN RUNNING. YOU MAY ALSO CHOOSE PEOPLE WHO SUPPORT YOU PERSONALLY OR PROFESSIONALLY. LIST THE PEOPLE IN YOUR SUPPORT NETWORK HERE:

CHOOSE ONE OF THE PEOPLE YOU LISTED ON THE PREVIOUS PAGE. WRITE SOME OF THE SPECIFIC WAYS THIS PERSON HAS ENCOURAGED OR INSPIRED YOU:

....

....

....

....

....

....

....

....

....

....

....

....

....

....

....

....

....

....

Does this person realize what she or he has meant to you? Consider writing a note or sending a text to express your gratitude.

Think about the ways that you can give and receive support. Perhaps you can commit to texting your running partner after each run and say, "Thanks for meeting me yesterday!" or "You kicked butt during our run this morning!" If you have a specific goal, be willing to ask someone in your network to help hold you accountable.

Social connections don't always come easy, and strong relationships don't form overnight. If you are new to an area or new to running, you might not yet have found a group. Get online and research local running groups, or connect to other runners using social media. You can start by connecting with me on Instagram (@karagoucher). I am constantly inspired by the amazing women who I meet and connect with online.

confidence essays

I am excited to share perspectives from six inspirational women, each of whom has supported me in my journey.

· · ·· ··· ·· · · ··· · · · · · · ·· ···· ·· · · ··· · · · · · ·· · · ·· · · · · · · · · · · · · · ·· ·

| MOLLY HUDDLE | SALLY BERGESEN | ROBIN ARZÓN |
| EMMA COBURN | CHRISTY TURLINGTON BURNS | MARY WITTENBERG |

confidence essays

I RELY ON THE STRENGTH of my relationships for support and inspiration in my running (as well as in the rest of my life). While certain confidence techniques have worked at different points in my career, my social connections are a constant.

My family, friends, training partners, coaches, and many other people form the support network on which I rely. They support and sustain me in countless ways. If you are a female runner reading this book, chances are that you've already discovered a certain little secret: women who run form a powerful, supportive community. It's a fact. We have each other's backs. We lift each other up when we're down, and we celebrate each other's successes—and we're there for all of the moments in between.

When I began this book project, it was natural for me to reach out to my community to share what I was working on. While I was very excited and motivated by the immediate positive feedback I received, I was humbled and touched when a number of women whom I admire agreed to lend their support in more tangible ways. You see, each of these women has a story to share about building confidence.

What I began to realize, however, is that each woman's story is also unique to her. Isn't that amazing? I notice that for women, arriving at a place of confidence is a singular journey, although many of the mile markers can be similar. I was seized by the urge to share not only my story, but the stories of several of the remarkable women I know.

In the following pages, you'll hear from athletes, mothers, businesswomen, and more. Each one graciously shares her wisdom and her own experience of building confidence. I hope that you are inspired by these strong, incredible women, just as I am. ❧

MOLLY HUDDLE

2012 + 2016 SUMMER OLYMPICS PARTICIPANT
AMERICAN RECORD HOLDER: 10,000 METERS AND HALF MARATHON

I've been told I'm in the category of people with a "quiet confidence."

I was always afraid of being cocky, because it's just not something I'm comfortable with. I know it can be entertaining to watch a brazen athlete point beyond the outfield or hype up a big future performance, but like a risqué piece of fashion, it's just not something I can pull off. That's for ballers and boxers and pop stars, I thought. It requires a larger-than-life personality and a penchant for showmanship that I just do not have. The constant inauthenticity it would take to fake my dweeby, distance-runner way just stressed me out.

I've come to realize you can have the confidence that is essential to success without being cocky, because they are very different.

I view confidence as belief in yourself. However, it's an inner dialogue that's not necessarily connected to what you outwardly say or show.

The major source of my confidence is work.

I feel confident from the workload I put in while training, knowing it is both the cornerstone of all good performances and a predictor of what realm of performance is possible for me.

This is not to say I give myself limits. I just think hitting a big performance target requires a certain level of accuracy on what exactly you're trying to do.

"THE MAJOR SOURCE OF MY CONFIDENCE IS WORK. I FEEL CONFIDENT FROM THE WORKLOAD I PUT IN WHILE TRAINING, KNOWING IT IS BOTH THE CORNERSTONE OF ALL GOOD PERFORMANCES AND A PREDICTOR OF WHAT REALM OF PERFORMANCE IS POSSIBLE FOR ME."

My training journals are both a guide and a source of mental strength.

Recording miles and workouts and reading them before races helps calm irrational fears and keeps me focused on the task at hand. This reminds me that I'm prepared, and prevents me from becoming too distracted by uncontrollable factors.

I think being open-minded and trusting your ability to learn and improve are also reflections of being confident.

Sometimes when I get discouraged I ask myself these questions:

Are you really giving yourself the best shot?

What could be better?

How can I get out of my own way?

Who can help me look at things differently?

What do I need to let go of and what do I need to adopt?

Because ultimately, I see confidence as believing in yourself enough to give you and your dreams the best shot.

It's a willingness to put in the work, learn from mistakes, and seek guidance from mentors and experts because you trust that you really CAN hit your goals with these ingredients.

Also, with confidence, you enter into the contract of uncertainty implicit in all dream-chasing because you believe you will make it all worthwhile.

"...WITH CONFIDENCE, YOU ENTER INTO A CONTRACT OF UNCERTAINTY IMPLICIT IN ALL DREAM-CHASING BECAUSE YOU BELIEVE YOU WILL MAKE IT ALL WORTHWHILE."

It's not that you know you won't drop the ball, or that you will win the gold.

No one knows that for sure.

It's that you know you will be okay, win or lose. It's a kind of fearlessness this way.

In fact, you have to know it will be more than okay, because you have to realize the process as a whole will make you better/stronger/tougher/wiser/more alive. That view has emboldened me on the track in ways I wouldn't have predicted from my non-running life. Racing has pushed me to cultivate a form of confidence that suits me best. It's not the loudest message but I can hear it, and more importantly, I've learned to listen to it. **MH**

EMMA COBURN

2017 WORLD CHAMPION AMERICAN RECORD HOLDER IN 3000M STEEPLECHASE
FIRST AMERICAN WOMAN TO WIN AN OLYMPIC MEDAL IN STEEPLECHASE
2016 OLYMPIC BRONZE MEDALIST

Confidence is earned. That is something my husband, who is also my coach, tells me. We work to earn the confidence we have on race day. Without the work, it's just smoke and mirrors.

I wasn't always a confident athlete. I grew up with two older siblings who were both more athletic and more outgoing than me. I was the runt of the litter who did her best to tag along with the big kids. I was never the athlete, the fastest, the strongest, or bravest. Trying to keep up with my older siblings paid off eventually, because as I entered my adolescent years, my athletic abilities started blossoming. But my confidence took longer to bloom. I was a leader and a captain, but when I ran, I would still go to the

"THE FEELING OF KNOWING I HAVE DONE EVERYTHING POSSIBLE TO BE MY BEST DIRECTLY TRANSLATES TO MY CONFIDENCE ON THE STARTING LINE."

starting line scared. Scared of failure, scared of the hurt, and scared of the worst possible outcome. One such instance was in my junior year of high school at the state cross country meet where I began crying on the starting line. Overwhelmed with nerves, I felt unsure of myself and out of my element, like I wasn't good enough or capable of handling the challenge of the race.

Then, in college at the University of Colorado, I started training. REALLY training. I started training harder and smarter than I ever had before. I worked hard, logged miles, got fit, took care of my body in the gym, and got treatment. I was prepared. My confidence grew. I was pushed to work harder than I thought possible. My consistent efforts in practice made the races less intimidating. I had big workouts under my belt that simulated the challenge of races. My mindset was shifting. My hard work bred confidence.

Before races there are still nerves, but the nerves are feelings of excited anticipation and not fear. I was more nervous standing on the starting line for a track meet in high school than I was for the World Championships as a pro runner. I can now stand on the starting line, take a few deep breaths, and know I am prepared. The feeling of knowing I have done everything possible to be my best directly translates to my confidence on the starting line.

True confidence can't be faked. You may be able to fake some confidence on the outside, but the feeling of true confidence must be earned. True belief in oneself comes with patient work, day in and day out. It comes with surrounding yourself with people who believe, and push and challenge you, but who ultimately are your biggest cheerleaders. **EC**

"TRUE BELIEF IN ONESELF COMES WITH PATIENT WORK, DAY IN AND DAY OUT."

SALLY BERGESEN

CEO & FOUNDER, OISELLE

In many ways, confidence is a Catch-22. It's hard to start things if we don't have it, but we won't gain confidence if we never begin. We need to give ourselves permission to fail.

What's important to know, however, is that the starting place and being without confidence is not only normal—it's shared by almost every high-achieving person you can think of. No one is born fully formed into their successes. Everyone starts at the beginning. And the condition is always the same: lack of knowledge. We haven't made valuable mistakes and don't yet grasp the complexity of what's to come. And we haven't put in the work.

"YOU WERE VULNERABLE, AND LEARNED, WORKED, AND HUSTLED YOUR WAY INTO A BETTER, MORE KNOWLEDGEABLE SPACE. AND THAT SHOULD MAKE YOU FEEL VERY CONFIDENT."

But once you do, confidence will come. It. Will. Come.

And when it does, it will be with you forever. Because once you've achieved a goal, your internal bar gets reset at a higher point. And even if you go back to the starting place say, in a different field or pursuit, you'll know that you were there before. You were vulnerable, and learned, worked, and hustled your way into a better, more knowledgeable space.

And THAT should make you feel very confident. **SB**

CHRISTY TURLINGTON BURNS

FOUNDER & CEO, EVERY MOTHER COUNTS

The moment I knew I was the mother of a daughter, I knew what I wanted most for her. It's what I want for every girl, woman, and mother: confidence.

Giving birth to my daughter was a pivotal moment in my life and probably the most life-transforming, confidence-boosting event for me still to this day.

I had complete confidence in my body's capacity to go through the physiological process of birth. I had created a birth plan and had access to quality and respectful maternity care. I also had the support of an incredible team who respected my wishes and did all they could to give me the experience I wanted and had worked so hard to achieve. I had my heart

and mind set on an unmedicated birth. That was my goal. So, I prepared myself as best I could and trained hard for a goal I had set for myself.

I will never forget my midwife asking my tolerance level. Had I run a marathon? Had I climbed a mountain? When in my life had I needed to dig as deep as I would need to, to give birth? When I finally did run my first marathon several years later, I understood what she meant. When you achieve a spiritual, physical, and mental goal, it's a whole other level.

Even with all that planning, things did not go exactly as I imagined. I experienced a postpartum complication that then led me to follow a path I have been on since, advocating for safe and respectful maternity care for every mother, everywhere.

My vision is a world where every woman has the opportunity to enter motherhood and not only survive, but also thrive. **CTB**

"WHEN YOU ACHIEVE A SPIRITUAL, PHYSICAL, AND MENTAL GOAL, IT'S A WHOLE OTHER LEVEL."

ROBIN ARZÓN

NEW YORK TIMES BEST-SELLING AUTHOR OF **SHUT UP AND RUN**
ULTRAMARATHON ROCKSTAR

LETTER TO MY 10-YEAR OLD SELF

Start before you're ready. On a gut instinct, you'll book a flight (that costs more than rent) to the London Olympics to be a writer, just two weeks after quitting your successful legal career. That trip will change your life.

For a kid who forged notes to get out of gym, you're going to run a lot—a dumb amount. It's going to become your life's work as a coach and ultramarathoner to run more miles than your brain can compute. You will redefine who an athlete is and help others do it, too. You'll decide to run five marathons in five days to raise money for multiple sclerosis research. It will change you.

"TRUST YOUR STRUGGLE. IT'S NOT ALWAYS SUPPOSED TO FEEL COMFORTABLE."

1. **Trust your struggle.**
   It's not always supposed to feel comfortable. Growth lives in the climb.

2. **Write your story using fear as fuel.**
   Does it get your blood pumping? Does it make you nervous? Then that's the challenge you were meant to encounter. Your passions are not accidental. Pursue them.

3. **Listen to the little voice inside.**

   Your body unlocks passion and potential. Honor it with sweat. Create laugh lines. Screw the stretch marks you've had since puberty. They are your warrior stripes. The key to your power is the flame in your belly.

4. **Superheroes are real.**

   Seek out those who fan your flames. Surround yourself with people who make you proud and humbled in their presence.

5. **Let things go.**

   You have to put what weighs you down to fly. Put the bags down. Those wounds are not your story. Ask yourself: will this matter in a month, or a year? A decade? Lighten your load. You are not baggage claim.

6. **Do epic sh*t.**

   Dream so big that it scares you. Shock yourself with what your body can do. Take up more space in this world. People need to witness boldness, personified.

   Create yourself every moment. You and only you are responsible for your happiness. Life is happening right now. This isn't a dress rehearsal.

7. **Fail bigger.**

   Failure is feedback. Failure means progress. The people who haven't failed, haven't lived. You're in for a real life "Choose Your Own Adventure." Make it spectacular. Manifest thoughts into things with action.

Sit on the porch swing in 50 years with salacious, powerful, inspiring, goosebumps-inducing stories to tell. Learn the power of "no." Own your "yes."

Above all, do more of what makes you happy. Sometimes, it really is that simple.

Xx. RA

"FAIL BIGGER. FAILURE IS FEEDBACK. FAILURE MEANS PROGRESS."

MARY WITTENBERG

FORMER PRESIDENT AND CEO, NEW YORK ROAD RUNNERS
1987 MARINE CORPS MARATHON WINNER

Reminders that boost my confidence when I need it:

My confidence comes from MY desire to do this.

When it gets hard, I remember, I am the one who wants this.

When I hate moments, I know it will be worth it.

Nothing extraordinary has ever been guaranteed.

Race pace: I have done this before. Just in increments. I can string this together.

Mind over matter. Always.

"FOCUS ON EFFORT."

Nerves are normal. Overcoming them is a superpower. I've got it.

What's the worst thing that can happen?

My experience matters. It gives me confidence.

I am contributing my whole being. The best I have today.

In race and in challenge, I try to take it moment by moment. I don't get ahead of myself.

Focus on effort. I never know what's changing around me. Opportunities can open up when we least expect them.

Stay focused on goals. **MW**

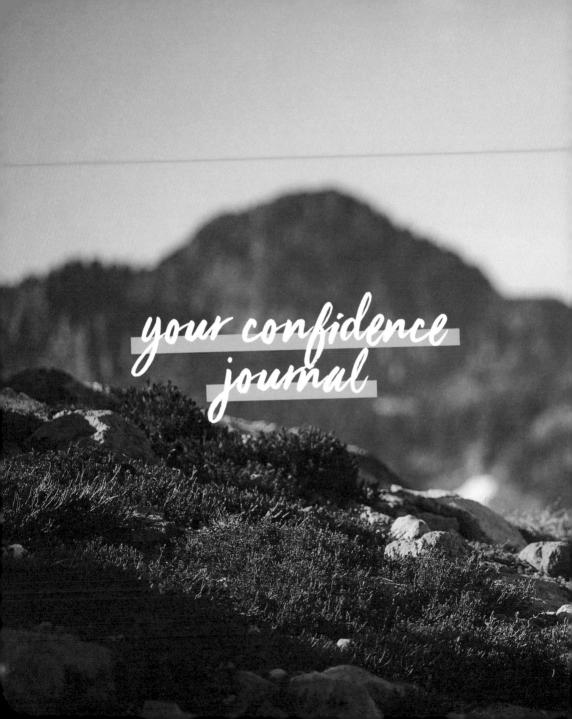

your confidence
journal

YOU HAVE MADE IT THIS FAR—CONGRATULATIONS!

I started this book project because I wanted to share my own practice of keeping a confidence journal, and what that has meant in my own training. I soon realized that there was so much more to share, and the book evolved into what you now hold in your hands. It is my deep hope that you have been inspired to learn about confidence, and that you have also learned about yourself. Here's the thing: there is always, always something new to discover about yourself.

That is what this final section of the book is about. It's about continuing your beautiful story. It's about continuing to learn, to challenge yourself, to grow into an even more amazing version of you.

As I said way back at the beginning, my confidence journal has been a vital tool. I use my own confidence journal as a companion to my training journal. In my training journal, I log the crucial information about my workout each day. In my confidence journal, however, I jot down thoughts about how I feel about each run.

A confidence journal entry doesn't have to take a lot of time, but it shouldn't be overly vague. Rather, it should help you to put a positive focus on what you have done—even if your run was difficult. It is important for your journal entry to be precise enough that you can look back months later and recall that specific workout. Here again are a couple of examples that I shared in the early pages of this book:

8/9   Feeling really bad and stiff from traveling. Doing 3x1 mile laps and after 2 had option to stop. Decided to go and ended up fastest one!

10/19   Amazing 18 mile run and 1 cool down. Literally had to hold myself back at times and never slowed a bit. In the last ⅓ of run-in fact gained time there. 6:07 average and HR 156. So close to being ready.

Having written this book, I can tell you (with confidence!) that sometimes staring at a blank page can be the scariest part of writing down your thoughts. To help you get started, the following few pages are filled with prompts to get you used to the types of things you might want to write about.

Now, I've never really been a "Dear Diary" kind of woman, but I want to assure you on one important point: there is not a wrong (or right) way to write a confidence journal entry. Just hang in there and it will begin to feel less uncomfortable and more natural as it becomes a part of your daily routine. If you feel uncomfortable or experience resistance, it doesn't mean that you should stop. Rather, I believe this is a sign of growth. ✔

BE CONFIDENT

BE WELL

STRONG!

I HOPE YOU WILL SHARE YOUR CONFIDENCE JOURNEY!

#STRONGWITHKARA

WHICH MANTRA DID YOU USE TODAY? HOW DID IT HELP?

WHAT DID YOU THINK ABOUT DURING YOUR RUN TODAY?

WHICH AREAS OF YOUR RUNNING ARE IMPROVING?

(kindness to yourself, speed, strength, sleep, nutrition, recovery)

WHAT IS SOMETHING THAT DID NOT GO YOUR WAY TODAY?
HOW DID YOU PUSH THROUGH IT?

WHAT IS ONE THING YOU DID TODAY THAT HELPED
YOU TO PREPARE FOR YOUR RACE OR TO MEET YOUR
NEXT BIG GOAL?

REFLECT ON YOURSELF ONE YEAR AGO. HOW HAVE YOU
IMPROVED AND GROWN SINCE THEN?

WHAT DID YOU FIGHT THROUGH TODAY THAT YOU DIDN'T
THINK YOU COULD?

WHAT FELT GREAT TODAY? DID IT SURPRISE YOU?

WHAT WAS THE BEST PART OF TODAY? WHAT WAS THE
WORST PART, AND HOW DID YOU PUSH THROUGH IT?

WRITE DOWN ONE POSITIVE WORD THAT EXPLAINS YOUR
RUN TODAY. WHY DID YOU CHOOSE THAT WORD?

WHAT IS ONE THING THAT IS MOTIVATING YOU RIGHT NOW?

HAVE YOU OVERCOME ANY CHALLENGES LATELY?

LIST ONE REASON THAT YOU ARE GOOD ENOUGH TO MEET
YOUR BIG GOAL.

WRITE ONE POSITIVE SENTENCE ABOUT YOURSELF.

NAME SOMEONE WHO BELIEVES IN YOU.
WHY DO THEY BELIEVE IN YOU?

WHAT HAVE YOU LEARNED THIS TRAINING CYCLE THAT HAS
MADE YOU A BETTER RUNNER?

LIST ONE THING THAT YOU WERE REALLY
GOOD AT TODAY.

WRITE ABOUT ONE THING THAT HAPPENED TODAY THAT
BROUGHT YOU JOY.

WRITE ABOUT ONE WAY THAT YOU INVESTED IN YOUR RUNNING PERFORMANCE TODAY.

HOW DID YOU CONTINUE TO TRY WHEN THE ODDS WERE AGAINST YOU?

WRITE ABOUT A GOOD CHOICE THAT YOU MADE TODAY.

LIST ONE THING YOU LOVED ABOUT YOUR RUN TODAY.

LIST SOMETHING THAT HAPPENED TODAY THAT WAS BETTER THAN YESTERDAY.

DID YOU CHOOSE TO BE CONFIDENT AND BELIEVE IN YOURSELF TODAY?

LIST THREE REASONS YOU ARE GRATEFUL FOR RUNNING.

LIST THREE REASONS WHY YOU ARE A STRONG RUNNER.

WHAT IS AN AREA OF YOUR RUNNING THAT YOU ARE STRUGGLING WITH? CAN YOU COME UP WITH ONE REASON THAT YOU ARE GRATEFUL FOR THIS STRUGGLE?

DID YOU LEARN ANY LESSONS DURING YOUR RUN TODAY?

I HOPE THAT THESE PROMPTS HELPED YOU to reflect on your running and your confidence. I encourage you to continue your confidence journal practice on your own. I have included some tips and provided a few pages for you to get started. Remember: this work is important and you are worth it!

Confidence Journal Tips:

1. You can use any notebook. If you do not like to keep track of a notebook, you can even use the notebook app on your phone!

2. Every day, after your workout, write down one thing that went well.

3. Make sure that your confidence journal entry is precise enough that you can flip through your journal months later and remember the exact workout.

4. The night before (or morning of) a big race or big training session, flip through your confidence journal. Remember all of the training that you did to get to this point. Remember all of the highs and the workouts that you nailed. Remember all of the times that you struggled, but then persevered.

5. Take in all of this positivity, and go with confidence to run your heart out. You are STRONG!

DATE _____

DATE _____

DATE _____

DATE _____

DATE _____

DATE _____

DATE _____

DATE _____

DATE _____

DATE _____

DATE _____

DATE _____

DATE _____

DATE _____

DATE _____

DATE _____

DATE _____

DATE _____

DATE _____

DATE _____

DATE _____

Thank you for allowing me to be a part of your running journey. I hope that what you learned in this book was valuable and that it will help you to grow as a runner and as a person. Now that you know how to keep a confidence journal, make your own. You can use any style of notebook, any size. Keep it in a place where you will remember to write in it (I leave mine on my bedside table, on top of my training journal).

Happy training!

ABOUT THE AUTHOR

Kara Goucher is a Midwest girl at heart, with the grit of New York City roots. Kara is a professional runner, mentor, proud mother, and loving wife. She graduated from the University of Colorado with three Division I NCAA championships in cross-country, the 3,000 meters, and 5,000 meters. She is a two-time Olympian, an American record holder, World Championships medalist, and one of the most accomplished female distance runners of all time.

In addition to her professional résumé, Kara is an inspiration to runners everywhere. She was named the "Most Recognizable Female Running Personality" by Run USA in 2015, and has been on the cover of *Runner's World Magazine* seven times— more than any other athlete. Kara leads her Podium Retreat each year, forming connections with other female runners. She is a passionate advocate for clean sport, healthy eating, fitness, and life balance.

accomplishments

TWO-TIME U.S. OLYMPIAN

Competed in the 5k and 10k in the 2008 Beijing Olympics, and the marathon in the 2012 London Olympics.

BOSTON MARATHON PODIUM FINISHER

Placed 3rd in 2009, the first time in 24 years that an American man and an American woman both appeared on the podium.

FASTEST-EVER AMERICAN WOMEN'S MARATHON DEBUT

NYC Marathon, November 2008—2:25:53—American course record at the time. Earned 3rd place and became the first American woman to finish in the top three in 14 years.

AMERICAN HALF-MARATHON RECORD HOLDER

Finished in a time of 1:06:57 at the 2007 Great North Run Half Marathon in Newcastle, England in September—recording the fastest-ever women's half marathon debut in the world—a distinction that still stands today.

WORLD CHAMPIONSHIPS SILVER MEDALIST

Placed 2nd at the World Track & Field Championships in 2007—the first and last time that a U.S. athlete, man or woman, medaled in the 10,000 meter in a world championship.

COLLEGIATE CROSS COUNTRY INDIVIDUAL & TEAM NCAA CHAMPION, UNIVERSITY OF COLORADO

2000—3,000 meter national champion, 5,000 meter national champion and cross country champion.

acknowledgments

This book means so much to me and it would have never come to life without the contributions of so many wonderful people.

First I'd like to thank Shanna Burnette, my dear friend and agent, and Brenna Dominguez, my editor at Blue Star Press, for helping to turn my vision and idea into to a real book.

Huge thank you to my friends Dr. Walker, Adrienne Langelier, Emma Coburn, Sally Bergesen, Christy Turlington Burns, Molly Huddle, Robin Arzón, and Mary Wittenberg. These incredible people shared their wisdom and personal experience throughout this book, and I know that the readers will enjoy their contributions as much as I have.

I would like to thank the Oiselle team and Jess Barnard for the beautiful photos in this book.

I am so grateful for my mom and my sisters. They are and have always been great examples of confident women and I have learned so much from them.

I'd like to thank Adam and Colt for their unwavering support of me and all of my dreams. They are always there for me in all of life's adventures.

I want to thank my coaches and teammates throughout the years who have always built me up when my confidence was lacking.

Also, I would like to express my love and gratitude to my fans. You have stuck with me throughout my career and you never cease to motivate and inspire me. I would not be who I am or where I am today without your support.

–KARA

references

Adam, H., & Galinsky, A. 2012. "Enclothed Cognition." Journal of Experimental Social Psychology 48: 1225-1398.

Carney, D., Cuddy, A., & Yap, A. 2010. "Brief nonverbal displays affect neuroendocrine levels and risk tolerance." Psychological Science.

Gabana, N., Steinfeldt, J. Wong Y., & Chung, B. 2016. "Gratitude, Burnout, and Sport Satisfaction Among College Student-Athletes: The Mediating Role of Perceived Social Support." Journal of Clinical Sport Psychology 11: 14-33.

Fleshman, L., McGettigan-Dumas, R. 2014. *Believe I Am Training Journal.*

Fleshman, Lauren. 2015. "How The Outside Affects The Inside." *Oiselle*, October 15, 2015. http://www.oiselle.com/blog/how-outside-affects-inside.

McCormick, A., Maijen, C., & Marcora, S. 2015. "Psychological Determinants of Whole-Body Endurance Performance." Sports Medicine 45: 997-1015.

Petrie, T. A., Deiters, J., & Harmison, R. J. 2014. "Mental toughness, social support, and athletic identity: Moderators of the life stress–injury relationship in collegiate football players." Sport, Exercise, and Performance Psychology 3 (1): 13-27.